About Pets

Dwarf Rabbit

A guide to selection, housing, care,
nutrition, behaviour, health, breeding,
species and colours

about pets

Contents

Contents

Foreword

When planning to buy a pet, it is very important to
gather plenty of information, even if it is only a small
animal such as a dwarf rabbit. Does the pet fit into
your family? How much work is day-to-day care and
what will it cost to buy, house and keep? Is the animal
happy to be cuddled, or does it prefer to be admired
from a distance? This book offers an overview of the
various breeds, their characteristics and their needs.
It aims to be a guideline for responsible care, which
includes various aspects of the dwarf rabbit's life. If
you plan to breed, this book can lead you on your first
steps in this gripping, versatile hobby.

This book is not a comprehensive reference book
about dwarf rabbits. We could fill a whole book just
with the different breeds, but you can find helpful
basic information here. What do you need to look
out for when buying an animal, for example? How is
a hutch built, and what does a dwarf rabbit eat?
Apart from general information such as origins,
history, buying, housing, behaviour, reproduction and
health, a brief description of hobby breeding and
sports is provided. A separate chapter is devoted to
the various breeds and colourings that characterise
the world of the dwarf rabbit.

About Pets

© 2009 About Pets bv
P.O. Box 26, 9989 ZG Warffum,
the Netherlands
www.aboutpets.info
E-mail: management@aboutpets.
info

ISBN: ISBN 9781852792114

First printing September 2003
Second printing December 2004
Third printing october 2005
Fourth revised printing 2006
Fifth revised printing 2007
Sixth printing 2009

Photos: About Pets photography
team

Acknowledgements:
Photos: Dick Hamer, Vitakraft and
Rob Doolaard

Dwarf rabbits are kept for three different reasons. Firstly as pets, then as exhibition animals or as experimental animals.

A large number of hobby-breeders keep (dwarf) rabbits to breed the prettiest examples or to develop new colourings or even new breeds. Dwarf rabbits are popular with many breeders because of their format. After all, ten English Lops naturally need a lot more space than ten dwarfs. Sadly, rabbits still occupy first position when it comes to animal experiments. New Zealand Whites are mostly used for this purpose in the UK.

This book is about the dwarf rabbit as a pet. These mini-rabbits with their pretty appearance are especially popular and are mainly kept by children. This doesn't mean they're some kind of cuddly toy – they can have quite a will of their own!

Compared to a normal rabbit, many people prefer the dwarf varieties. They need a smaller hutch (and thus less shavings and straw) and eat less.

Origins
Like all rabbit varieties, the dwarf rabbit originates from the common European wild rabbit. It is a mammal but, in contrast to what many believe, it is not a rodent! Rabbits belong to the family of the hares (Lagomorpha). Hares and rabbits have four rather than two incisor teeth in the upper jaw and, behind the long incisors, there are two small teeth in the upper jaw.

The widespread misunderstanding that rabbits and hares belong to the rodent order (Rodentia) has not been just a result of speculation. Originally, the "long-eared" were classified among the rodent order. However, scientific research and fossils later made it clear that hares and rabbits are not related at all to the rodents. Looking back into the very distant past, it even appears that the hares have more in common with hoofed animals.

The earliest ancestors of the hare appear to date from the cretaceous period. One assumes that these were insect eaters from the Pseudictops gender. These developed into the ancestors of the hares and rabbits we know today.

The order of the hare-likes consists at the moment of approximately twenty types of hare, thirty types of rabbit and ten types of Pika (Rock Rabbit). Apart from the Pika, all varieties look similar. They all look very much like their ancestors. They are spread over practically the whole world, and live in many different climates.

Many sorts of animals have adapted to changes in climate and habitats. Hares and rabbits have not changed very much and they still show many primitive characteristics.

It seems that these animals are capable of surviving almost anywhere without having to adapt. The hares have, however, like almost all animals in the wild, adapted to their environment with the colour of their coat. It is white in the snow, yellow-grey in the prairie and dark in the forests.

Hare family members are found almost anywhere in the world, from the North Pole to Australia. The only places where they are not found are the South Pole, Madagascar, parts of Indonesia and the southern part of South America. Wild hares generally have primitive brains, which means that they are not particularly intelligent. They compensate for this with highly developed hearing and an excellent sense of smell. Only a few varieties make noises. They vary in length and weight from twelve centimetres and one hundred grams to seventy centimetres and seven kilos.

Rodent Incisors

One of the very few things rodents and rabbits have in common are their rodent incisors. Rabbits, like rodents, have constantly growing incisors without roots. There are two in the upper and two in the lower jaw. These teeth are extremely strong, but do get worn down by their constant gnawing.

Pet dwarf rabbit

Nature has found a solution: the teeth keep growing, the whole life long. There is, however, a disadvantage to this. If the upper and lower teeth no longer fit properly onto each other, due to a deformed jaw or a hard knock, they are no longer 'stopped' by the opposite tooth. They grow unchecked and sometimes even into the opposite jaw. You can read more about this in the chapter 'Health'.

Differences

Although both belong to the hare-family, the hare and the rabbit are fundamentally different animals, not only in appearance, but also in reproduction and behaviour. The European hare is much bigger and heavier than the European rabbit, and it also has longer ears.

The hare is a long distance runner, which can jump very high, whereas the rabbit is a very flexible sprinter. Hares make a nest on the ground (lair), and they are also found in the mountains. Rabbits, on the other hand, dig burrows and prefer flat land. Hares live solitary lives and look for a partner only when they want to reproduce. Rabbits live in big groups. Hares mate in full run, whereas rabbits mate in a sitting position. Hares give birth to two to four young after approximately 43 days, and the young can run and see straight away (precocial). Rabbits give birth to more young

Wild rabbit

(up to twelve) after some 30 days. Their young are naked, deaf and blind when born (nestling).

The European wild rabbit

As mentioned above, all the (dwarf) rabbit breeds descend from the European wild rabbit. This rabbit has a chocolate-grey colouring, which can be very uneven. The belly is white. The tail is almost black on top, and white underneath. This pattern is referred to as 'Agouti', after the South American cavy-like rodent. The body is 35 to 50 centimetres long, the tail 4 to 8 centimetres and the ears 6.5 to 7.3 centimetres. Their weight varies between 1.3 and 2.5 kilos.

The European wild rabbit is found in western and central Europe, from Spain to southern Sweden and from Ireland to Hungary. In Italy, it is only found in a few areas. Wild rabbits live in open landscape, such as fields, meadows, dunes, heather fields, and sometimes also in not too dense woods. They are not found in mountain regions above nine hundred metres. They prefer sandy ground.

Domestication

The Romans were the first to keep rabbits. They were not yet common in Italy during the Roman Empire. After the conquest of Spain, the Romans discovered how palatable rabbit flesh is.

They captured rabbits and took them home. There, they were released into the wild. Later, the Romans built special rabbit cages, the so-called leporaria, in which they could keep their rabbits.

In the Middle Ages, the rabbit was the favourite prey of the hunting elite. The animals were released onto small islands for that purpose. The Dutch zoologist Hans Nachtsheim did a lot of research into the domestication of the rabbit. He concluded that the first tame rabbits were bred in French monasteries. He based this on writings from the sixteenth century, in which different colourings are mentioned for the first time.

Domestication ensured that the tame rabbit soon differed from its wild cousins. The ears and eyes of the tame rabbit are not as efficient as those of the wild varieties, and it has 22 percent less brain. Tame rabbits can reproduce the whole year round, while their wild cousins can only give birth in the spring.

The Origins of
the Dwarf Rabbit
The first tame rabbits were bred to be as big as possible because that delivered more meat. At the same time, breeders tried to breed pretty colours so that the fur could be used for colourful coats.

Thus appeared the first colour varieties including snow white. These white rabbits were shipped from Poland to England. There, breeders tried to breed these animals as small as possible as a hobby.

So the first dwarf rabbits came from England where they were called "Polish" after their white Polish ancestors. Later it was mostly breeders in Holland, Germany and England who developed the various dwarf rabbit breeds. For example, the Netherland Dwarf Rabbit is a pure Dutch product which later became one of the most popular dwarf rabbits in the UK.

Polish
blue eyed

Although the dwarf rabbit is totally domesticated, its behaviour still reminds one of its wild compatriots in many respects.

Most striking is the so-called 'escape behaviour', which is very characteristic for rabbits. Just as their wild cousins, domestic dwarf rabbits are most active at night. When worried, they "thump" on the ground with their hind legs as an alarm signal. In the wild, rabbits raise the alarm in the same way whenever danger is nearby.

As a rabbit is usually nocturnal by nature, it is often very quiet during the day. It is not good for the animal to try to change this behaviour too much. It disturbs its natural rhythm.

A rabbit is a clean animal, even in the wild. You can find 'natural lavatories', where the animals go to the toilet every time. In captivity, a rabbit will always use the same corner of its cage.

Character
There are substantial differences in character between the various dwarf rabbit varieties. For example, the character of the Dwarf Lop can be described as charming. This trait is also true of the bigger lop rabbits. The Polish and true coloured dwarfs, however, can be really aggressive characters. Exhibition animals that have been bred largely for their appearance are not always loveable as pets. Pet shops will normally only sell friendly animals.

Behaviour

Company or cuddly toy

Some people buy a rabbit or another pet for their (small) children to play with. Live animals are, however, not toys. If you are looking for a cuddly toy for your children, buy one from a toyshop. However cute and soft a dwarf rabbit may be, you must not regard it as a cuddly animal. A rabbit will not be happy if it is constantly patted, brushed and played with by children's hands. It will allow itself to be cuddled, but make sure that you give it the opportunity to run freely. People with a garden may consider a shelter in the form of an outdoor run. The children can then enjoy watching their favourite pet, without constantly pestering it.

Children and dwarf rabbits

The above is not intended to prevent you from buying a rabbit for a child. Dwarf rabbits are generally excellent as 'children's animals'. When a young rabbit comes into the home, both children and rabbit have to get used to the new situation. The rabbit has to get used to being picked up by humans, while the children have to learn how to handle such a small animal. Let the children quietly hold their hand in the cage. The rabbit will sniff at it and maybe nibble at their fingers. Make very sure that the child does not jump and pull its hand back quickly when the rabbit nibbles at a finger or a fingernail. The animal might really bite when frightened. Because of their excitement about their new companion, children are often boisterous, while the rabbit is also agitated. It is therefore important to limit the attention for the new housemate, as it will need its rest too.

All too often, pets are bought on impulse. You're walking around a shopping centre with your children one Saturday and almost trip over a cage with cute dwarf rabbits. Before you know it, your family has a new housemate.

Obviously, this is not the ideal way to purchase a pet. It sometimes works out well, but more often it does not. Pets need a cage, food, medical care and anything else that adds up to care and attention, even when you come home after a tiring day at work, your children have to do homework, or a holiday is coming up.

A child is often enthusiastic at the prospect of having a pet and will promise faithfully to care for it.

Once the novelty has faded however, the parents often have to take over.

On the other hand, a pet in the house can be very rewarding. It brings life into the home, and a piece of nature. A dwarf rabbit is also usually a kind, affectionate little pet, which captures the hearts of adults and children alike. It is important that humans and animal suit each other. This is why you have to gather plenty of information in advance about keeping your favourite pet. What sort of cage does it need, what sort of climate, which food, what care, how much is it going to cost, have you got enough time? By answering all these questions before a possible purchase, you can prevent disappointments later. Never buy a pet if you are in any doubt.

One or more

If you want to buy a dwarf rabbit, one question then comes up: how many? Dwarf rabbits can easily be kept on their own. In this case, a female is an advantage. A buck can spread urine. This is also called 'spraying'. Males do this especially when they smell a female or have just mated one. If you want to keep several rabbits, think about it carefully. A male and female together will quickly have young. One nest of baby dwarf rabbits is certainly cute. But by the second or third time, all your neighbours, friends and family have already been supplied, and you cannot keep all the little ones yourself.

Just as male cats and dogs, a male dwarf rabbit can be neutered. This is, of course, expensive, and not every vet is willing to do such a "fiddly job".

If you do choose to buy a couple anyway, make sure that they are not related. If members of the same family reproduce, it is called in-breeding. This can cause damage to the young rabbits' health.

If you want two dwarf rabbits, but no young, choose two females. They are usually friendly towards each other. If two males have been together since birth, it usually does not cause any trouble. It is, however, common enough that adult males attack each other.

If you want to breed dwarf rabbits, it is a good idea to become a member of a small animal breeders club. There will be experienced breeders there, who are willing to help beginners with tips and advice.

The trick with the ears

If you buy a young dwarf rabbit without being certain that it's a purebred, you will never know how big the animal will become later. After all, there is no shortage of mongrel dwarf rabbits on sale.

A young rabbit bred from a dwarf and a normal rabbit may stay as small as a dwarf rabbit, but it can also become as large as a normal rabbit. To illustrate this, a fully grown dwarf rabbit can weigh some eight hundred to as much as sixteen hundred grams, while a fully grown

This rabbit will remain smaller ...

... than this rabbit

Dutch can weigh from two to three kilograms.

Fortunately close examination can help to estimate approximately how large a young rabbit will become. This is the trick with the ears. Young rabbits with long ears will usually grow large, while those with short ears will stay small.

Things to watch out for

When you go to buy a dwarf rabbit, look out for the following:

• The animal must be healthy. A healthy rabbit has clean, bright eyes, clean genitals, no unnatural lumps, a clean and dry nose, and clean lips without scabs.
• The fur should be smooth and shiny. There should be no wounds or flaking skin.
• The rabbit has to be well fed, but not fat. It should feel solid, but should not have a high back or hollow flanks.
• Pay attention to the breathing. Laboured or rattling breathing can be a sign of an infection.
• Droppings should be hard and dry. Pale, wet, soft droppings can be a sign of an (intestinal) infection.
• The rabbit should not be too young. During the suckling period, the young get substances from their mother that give them immunity they badly need. Always find out their age and never buy an animal younger than eight weeks.

Also, never buy an animal that seems too lightweight for its age.

• On the other hand, an animal should also not be too old. Older animals, of course, die sooner, but they also have more problems getting used to new surroundings. You can recognise older dwarf rabbits by their coat. It is often less glossy and sometimes displays bare patches.
• Also look at the other animals in the cage. If they look less lively or even sick, then the animal of your choice may also be harbouring an illness. Rabbits are vulnerable to infectious diseases.
• Try also to check that your animal is really the same sex as the salesperson told you. You can recognise full-grown males by their small testicles. A breeder can carefully press out a young male's penis.

Where to buy

There are several places to buy a dwarf rabbit. Most are sold in a pet shop. Generally, the rabbits sold there are of good quality. You need to be aware, however, that there are good and not-so-good pet shops. Therefore, take a good look around the shop. Are the cages clean? Are the animals on offer healthy and active?

Have they got plenty of clean drinking water? Do you get sufficient and, especially, honest information about the animals? Even if you have a good impression, it is still recommended to apply the trick with the ears. After all, it is a dwarf rabbit you're looking for.

There are many breeders of dwarf rabbits in the UK. These try to breed 'perfect' examples for shows. If they do not meet the strict competition rules, they are selected at a young age to be sold. These little animals are usually perfectly healthy, but may not be quite the right colour or build. Here too, it is important to be careful. There are some less good breeders around, who want their share of success. Your local small animal club will be able to give you addresses of trustworthy breeders.

Sadly, there is another type of breeder. These people try to breed as many animals as they can as fast as they can, in an attempt to get rich quick. Their 'victims' often live in draughty shelters, with little room. Inbreeding and disease are common. These breeders often offer their animals for sale via advertisements and on markets and car-boot sales. By buying from such people, you only help to keep such breeding factories running.

You can also buy a rabbit at one of the many breed shows, which are held primarily in the autumn and winter. Moreover, these shows are worth visiting even if you are not planning to buy a rabbit there.

Transport

If you are going to buy a dwarf rabbit, and you are well-prepared, you will probably take a transport box, a cage or a carton with you. Make sure that the animal is protected against draughts, rain and wind. It is stressful enough for the young rabbit: separation from the mother, the stay in the shop, and then going on another journey with an unknown destination. Leave it in peace as much as possible during the first few days. Give it the opportunity to get used to its new environment very slowly.

If you are picking your rabbit up with a car, do not let the animal stay in the hot sun while you go to do a quick errand. Even if the temperature outside does not seem high, it can get very warm in the car.

To be able to responsibly keep a dwarf rabbit as a pet, it's important to know how rabbits live in the wild. Even if your dwarf rabbit lives in a hutch or cage, it is still possible to get close to their natural habitat so that your pet will feel as comfortable as possible.

In the wild
Wild rabbits prefer to live in open areas and on sandy ground. They are very sociable animals, which live in big families. A rabbit family lives in a warren, and the bigger the family gets, the bigger the warren has to be.

The warren consists of the living room, from which a number of passages spread out.

These passages are divided into main passages and escape passages. The animals normally use the main passages, but in an emergency, such as an intruding weasel or ferret, for example, they choose the smaller emergency exits. One of the animals often looks for a higher point, from where it can spot danger.

Warrens are completely bare on the inside. The nesting chambers are quite a distance away from the living chamber. They are filled with dry grass, straw and fur, which the female plucks from her belly. After the birth, the mother visits the nesting chamber a few times a day to look after her young. After about thirty days the young leave the nesting chamber and integrate into the family.

Housing in captivity

You can keep your dwarf rabbits outdoors, but this is not advisable. You do not have as much contact with animals kept outdoors. The cage outside also has to be made resistant to the wet weather of our climate. Animals kept outdoors also seem not to live as long as animals kept indoors.

A shed is a good alternative. It is certainly the best for the animal. Your dwarf rabbit grows a nice thick winter coat in a draught-free shed. The air is also not too dry. Hobby breeders therefore always keep their animals in a shed or a stable. The pet rabbit owner has the disadvantage that a shed is still too far away from the living room. When it is raining, not everybody is happy to go outdoors. In this case, you also have too little contact with your rabbit, and it will feel lonely if it does not have others of its kind with it. A rabbit is an animal that does not like to be alone.

A place in the house might be the best solution. The kitchen, especially a small one, is not the right place, as animals cannot cope with cooking smells, especially the smoke of oil or butter. Many people also find it unhygienic. The hallway is also inadvisable, as it is too draughty. A bedroom that is also used for other purposes during the day is a good choice.

If the room is only used at night, the rabbit will feel lonely. The best place is the living room, however. As mentioned above, rabbits are very sociable animals. They like to be in our company. You have to pay good attention to a few things though:

- A rabbit does not like noise. Whether it's rock, classical, or other music, it is still noise to the sensitive ears of your rabbit. People who enjoy loud music should find another spot for their rabbit or wear headphones.
- Like most pets, rabbits do not like cigarette smoke. If people smoke in the living room, it is not the best place for your rabbit.
- The cage should not be in direct sunlight. The temperature can get extremely high, even in winter. Windows function like magnifying glasses.
- Draughts are lethal for rabbits. It is therefore best not to put the cage on the ground. A place on a box or a table is preferable. Put the cage against a wall or in a corner to guarantee as much peace and quiet as possible for your pet. The animal feels safe if 'its back is covered'.
- It should be obvious that a place next to an open fire or the central heating is also inadvisable.

At a hobby breeder's

Garden hutch

Cage types

Anyone with a bit of patience and DIY talent can build a cage himself. It is of course easier to buy one in the pet shop. It does not make a big difference in price;

the material for a DIY cage costs about the same as a ready-made example. The advantage of building a cage yourself is that you can adapt it completely to your own wishes and ideas. Have you got a corner of 90 by 45 centimetres between two cupboards?

You will have to search a long time for a cage to fit it. It can also be tricky to find the colour that will go perfectly with your interior.

Ready made cages in different sizes and styles are sold in pet shops and department stores. It is not always easy to decide. There are a few demands, which a rabbit cage should fulfil, even if you build it yourself:

• It should be a pleasant environment for the animal
• It must be big enough
• It must keep the animal contained
• There must be good air circulation
• Any mess should stay inside the cage
• It must be easy to clean
• It should be safe for animals and humans
• It must be easily accessible

A cage must be big enough for your animal. How big is big enough? Any cage is, really, a limitation to an animal's freedom, and is therefore never big enough. We must therefore find a good compromise between the needs of animal and human. The cage should not be too big for the human, but also not too small for the animal.

If your rabbit can regularly run around outside its cage, the following rule of thumb applies:

A grown animal must be able to lie alongside the short side of the cage, when it stretches out. The longer side of the cage is usually twice as long. For a pure dwarf rabbit this would result in 80 x 40 x 40 centimetres.

Take into account that a cross between a dwarf and a normal rabbit can get much bigger. Two dwarf rabbits, or one dwarf rabbit and a guinea pig (that can live together very happily) obviously need more space.

Obviously, a cage has to be strong enough to prevent escapes. The bars should therefore not be too far apart. Good ventilation is secured by gauze or bars at the sides of the cage. Solid glass tanks are therefore inadvisable. The ammonia fumes from the urine are trapped in the tank.

The sides of the bottom tray must be at least fifteen centimetres high to prevent too many droppings and shavings from falling out. However, you cannot completely prevent this from happening with rabbits.

To clean the cage thoroughly, you should be able to take it apart easily. There should also be no sharp protrusions on either the outside or inside. You also need to be able to take out the feed bowl without too much trouble.

If you follow all the advice above, you will probably choose a cage which consists of a plastic tray with a wire top. This top section should have a large door at the front, and a 'lid' that you can remove.

Do-it-yourself

If you do decide to build a cage yourself, you can use several techniques and materials. As an example, we will describe the construction of a simple rabbit hutch.

The hutch is made of plastic-covered chip board, approximately fifteen millimetres thick. You can buy this in any DIY store. You attach the side walls (48.5 x 45 centimetres) and the back wall (90 x 45 centimetres) to the floorboard (90 x 50 centimetres) with long, thin screws. At the bottom of the front wall, you attach a panel (87 x 15 centimetres) and a beam on the top (87 x 2 x 3 centimetres). Finally, you seal all seams with silicone, to prevent dampness getting into the components. The frame of the cage is now ready.

For the front, you need a frame, which you cover with gauze (87 x 27.5 centimetres). You close this front with three plugs in three holes at the bottom. You drill these holes into the top of the panel. At the top, the frame is kept in place by two pieces of wood, which you screw to the beam.

Two pieces at the sides of the frame, behind the front, prevent the frame from falling in. For the top, too, you make a frame, which you can take out (87 x 45 centimetres), which you cover with gauze. This is the lid of the cage. To prevent this lid from falling in, you attach six small metal plates at the sides. You can hang a water bottle at the front of the cage.

Cage litter

Wood shavings have been used in animal cages for many years. They are sometimes called sawdust, but are actually shavings. Shavings absorb moisture exceptionally well and hardly smell, but a major disadvantage is that they usually contain a lot of dust. Investigations in recent years have shown that this dust can seriously bother animals. There are now many other types of cage litter on the market that are "healthier" for animals.

Wood shavings

As we have said, shavings are not very suitable as cage litter. Rabbits seem to have fewer problems with the dust than some other pets. This is probably because wild rabbits, which always live on sandy ground, can more easily close their respiratory organs to keep out fine sand and dust.

Now that the dust problem has been generally recognised, some types of shavings are being cleaned more thoroughly by the

manufacturer. While wood shavings are thus not unsuitable by definition, a better material is preferable, even if this is often more expensive. But, in any event never use shavings from carpentry waste. They are often too fine in structure and may contain poisonous substances.

Hay

Rabbits like to use hay as nesting material and to chew on. It is an important part of their diet. Hay, however, does not absorb moisture well and is thus not really suitable as cage litter.

Straw

Straw is much too coarse to be suitable as cage litter or nest material for rabbits. There is a product on the market, which is made of shredded straw. Russel Rabbit is wonderfully soft and ideal as nesting material. However, it absorbs too little moisture to be really suitable as cage litter.

Cat litter

There are probably a hundred different sorts of cat litter on the market. Some are suitable to keep rabbits or other rodents on. These absorb plenty of moisture and can do good service. Cat litter made of stone or clay is less suitable, mainly because it can become dusty.

Pressed pellets

In recent years various cage litters have appeared on the market that

Wood shavings

consist of pressed pellets. Some types have sharp edges and don't seem very comfortable.

Sand

Sand absorbs too little moisture to be used as cage litter. Apart from that, it gets dirty.

Shredded paper

There are also various types of shredded paper on offer as cage litter. These shreds are ideal to play with and can be used as nest material. But they absorb much too little moisture to be used as cage litter. Never make cage litter yourself from old newspapers. The printing ink can poison rabbits. In conclusion, use a cage litter that easily absorbs moisture, in combination with a soft, insulating nesting material.

Interior

A rabbit cage must also contain a rack for its hay, which you can also buy ready-made at a pet shop. Water should be given in a drinking bottle that you hang on the outside, with the spout pointing into the cage. There are two small steel balls in the spout and by moving these the rabbit gets water.
Any rabbit will quickly get used to a drinking bottle.
Use a heavy stone dish for dry food. Rabbits like to stand at the dish with their forepaws on the edge. A dish that is too light will then easily tip over. Green food

can simply be laid in the cage.
It's a good idea to lay a piece of stone (paving slab) in the rabbit's regular running area. As the rabbit walks over it, it wears down its nails naturally.

Rabbits are clean animals that will pick their own toilet corner. Clean this corner every couple of days, then you will only need to clean the whole cage out every two weeks or so. Use an empty can to scrape the toilet corner clean. You can also put a flat littertray in this corner.
Your rabbit will then learn that the tray is where it is expected to do its business and then you only need to clean out the tray.

Running free

A pet that is reasonably tame and kept in a smallish cage needs to be let out regularly for a run. Sufficient exercise is very important for an animal's health. If you let your rabbit run in the house, garden or balcony, you need to be aware of some dangers. Watch out for electric cables that an animal may gnaw on, poisonous houseplants, doors that may suddenly slam shut as well as dogs. Always keep a good eye on an animal running free.

Hay with herbs

The European wild rabbit enjoys a comprehensive menu. What's on offer depends on its habitat and the season. The whole year round, it likes to eat grasses, young twigs, leaves, and other pieces of plants.

Depending on the season, the menu may include fruits, berries, fungi, and buds. Very exceptionally, the wild rabbit eats animals, such as beetles. The changes of seasons ensure the necessary variety in its menu, and also ensure that changes in the diet do not happen too quickly. For our domesticated rabbits, a comprehensive menu is also important. A good diet consists of a certain amount of basic ingredients: hay, dry food, fresh food and water. You might add some special treats.

Hay

Hay is an important element in a healthy rabbit's diet. Although it contains little in terms of nutrients, it's indispensable for the digestion. A dwarf rabbit must have fresh hay available every day. Apart from the all so important fibre, it also contains calcium and magnesium.
You can buy a bale of hay from a farmer or seed merchant, or smaller packages from a pet shop.

Good, fresh hay contains young grass, clover and herbs. It is dry, but still a little green and smells wonderful. Poor quality hay contains practically no herbs, because it's often harvested from barren meadows. You can recognise old hay by its yellowish colour. It also gives off dust, which can be

Nutrition

especially harmful to your animal's bronchial tracts. Apart from that, old hay contains no more nutrients.

Dry foods

Dry food is a collective name for any food that is not fresh: loose grain types, mixed grain with grass kernels and ready-made pellets. You can buy maize, grain, barley, yeast, millet and various seeds at seed merchants.

However, it's not worth the bother mixing your rabbit's food yourself. Ready-made rabbit grain mixtures contain everything your animal needs for a balanced diet. These mixed foods also contain grass pellets. Experience shows that rabbits eat these pellets last, so it's important that they get precisely the amount of food that they eat in one day. If anything is left over, give them somewhat less the next day.

There are also ready-made pellets in the shops. These pellets are all identical in their composition. They contain all the necessary nutrients and provide a perfect diet, without having to find and wash green vegetables. But apart from the ease of use, it must be pretty boring for a rabbit to have to eat the same food every day. It also doesn't match the European wild rabbit's varied diet.

Seeds and grains have a high nutritional value. A dwarf rabbit that gets too much mixed grain and too little green food and exercise can quickly get fat. In that case you can happily let your pet 'fast' one or two days a week. Only give it hay and water on these days. Whatever food you choose, always check the date of manufacture. Food that is older than three months loses a large portion of its nutritional value.

Green foods

Rabbits in the wild eat more green foods than grain, so green foods must make up a substantial part of the diet for a pet rabbit. Here we mean those green foods that are suitable for a (dwarf) rabbit. This list is almost inexhaustible, but never take a risk if in any doubt. Only give your rabbit things that you're sure it can eat.

You can find wild herbs in woods and meadows. Don't pick green foods for your pet alongside roads or in areas with heavy industry, as these plants are probably contaminated with lead and other poisons. Also avoid agricultural land, because of insecticides. To avoid any risk, wash any green food thoroughly, then let it drain and dry a little.

You can give your rabbit practically any fruit or vegetable, although some cabbage varieties

Water bottle

Licking block

can cause intestinal problems. Greenhouse lettuce contains a lot of nitrate, so give cabbage and lettuce only in small quantities.

Carrots are the most commonly known rabbit food, but too many can cause diarrhoea. Do not feed a rabbit more than one carrot per day. It is the rule for most fresh food that too much can cause problems.

Water

That dwarf rabbits need only a little to drink is a fable. Even if you give them plenty of green food, they still need fresh water every day. Give them water at room temperature in a drinking bottle. Clean the bottle regularly as poisonous algae can build up inside it. Rabbits sometimes have the habit of drinking from their bottle with a mouth full of food, so it can

become dirty or blocked. Check the bottle and replace the water every day.

Ten golden rules for good feeding

1. A rabbit cannot decide itself how much and what it has to eat and can become very fat very quickly. It can hardly or never detect poisonous food.
2. A varied menu is very important. This ensures that your rabbit gets plenty of nutrients.
3. Just as humans do, rabbits also like to eat regularly. They prefer to eat twice a day (dry food in the morning and fresh food in the evening).
4. Wash all fresh food and let the water drain off.
5. Remove any fresh food and fruit which has not been eaten within half an hour. It will go mouldy and litter the cage.

Suitable fresh food	Vegetables	Fruit
Field plants	Carrots	Apple
Dandelion leaves	Carrot leaves	Pear
Clover	Field lettuce	Banana
	Endives	Kiwifruit
Plantain	Chicory	Raspberry
	White radish leaves	Strawberry
Thistle	Celery	Grapes
	Kohlrabi	Cherries
Plucked grass	Fennel	Plums
	Sunflower seeds	
Young stinging nettles	Parsley	
	Spinach	
Jerusalem Artichoke	Corn on the cob	

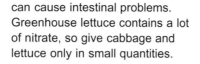

Pet shops carry a large assortment of snacks for your pet

6. Never collect fresh food at the sides of roads.
7. Beware of possible agricultural chemicals.
8. Never feed frozen or cooked food.
9. Avoid changing your rabbit's menu too quickly.
10. A good diet consists of hay, mixed grains, fresh food, water and something to gnaw on. This will ensure that your rabbit stays healthy.

Snacks and treats

Although the rabbit is not a rodent, it does have incisors. To keep its teeth in good condition it needs something to gnaw on. There are various munchies available in pet shops, but you can also use branches or twigs from willow, fruit or other deciduous trees. A hard slice of dried bread or some crispbread are equally suitable snacks.

Don't give a rabbit crisps, biscuits, sweets or sugar lumps as extras. These snacks are extremely unhealthy for pets, as they contain too much salt, sugar and fat. There are enough healthy snacks that you can use to give your dwarf rabbit a treat. Of course, not every animal has the same tastes, one rabbit may like something that another won't eat, but parsley, chicory, carrot leaves, rose-hips and kiwifruit will usually bring a smile to their faces. With a well-balanced diet, you don't need to add any extra vitamins or minerals. But it is a good idea to give rabbits a so-called salt-stone or licking block. They will use them automatically if they're lacking salt or minerals.

Hotot marking

Many people breed dwarf rabbits as a hobby. They take them to small-animal shows, where they hope to win prizes with their finest examples, but the pure-bred dwarf rabbit's appearance, colour and coat are subject to strict rules; not everything is permitted.

The perfect rabbit fulfils the standards of the breeders' association. Purebred rabbits shown in the UK must have a ring on their back leg from the British Rabbit Council, to prove that they are eligible. Rabbits without rings may only be shown in pet classes.

The Standard
The breeders' association standard describes how rabbits and other small rodents such as the guinea pig, the golden hamster, the mongolian gerbil and the tame rat or fancy mouse should ideally look.

Dwarf rabbits come in many more colourings and markings than those included in the standard. But a colouring or marking is only officially recognised if it's in the standard. For example, chocolate and yellow dwarf rabbits are described in the standard. If a breeder enters a dwarf rabbit that is not chocolate (like plain chocolate) and also not yellow, but some sort of medium brown, the animal does not fulfil the requirements and will receive a mediocre or poor score in the "Colour" category.

Dwarf Rabbit

One will judge the animal as a "poor" chocolate or yellow dwarf rabbit. It is also possible to enter the animal as a 'new colour' for the standard. Not every form of mixture of two colours will automatically be accepted in the standard. There are a number of requirements that a colour or marking must meet to be included. The first step is preliminary recognition. If, after three years, there are enough animals with the new colour or marking, it is then fully recognised.

Judging

During judging, the animals entered are judged on the following points:

Type and build

This part of the standard describes a dwarf rabbit's build. This is again different for each breed. You can read more about the various breeds, colourings and markings in the chapter "Breeds and colourings".

Weight

Before a show, dwarf rabbits can be entered in two categories: under 5 months and adult. When judging an animal's weight, its age category is taken into account.

A fully grown coloured dwarf rabbit or Polish may weigh maximum one kilogram.

Chocolate

Agouti

The judging

Black

Black and tan

Eight hundred grams is the lower limit.
A fully grown Holland Lop may weigh between 1250 and 1650 grams.

Coat and hair condition
This part of the standard varies per variety and hair structure. A show animal must have a full coat, laid flat and glossy, that means no thin or bald patches. Any moulting costs points and can be recognised by lack of guard hairs. These are the harder support hairs that are shed first. The new coat, which is longer and more intense in colour, is clearly visible. A few loose hairs are not a problem, but loose lumps are marked as moulting.

Head and ears
This section is also judged per variety and markings. You can find more details in the chapter "*Breeds*".

Topcoat and belly colour
The topcoat is understood to be the surface colour on the animal's back. The word 'surface' is very important here. A hair usually consists of different colours. The base of a hair (at the body) will have a certain colour (the base colour). The tip of the hair then has the top or belly colour. In certain cases, in Agouti patterned rabbits for example, the intermediate part of the hair will have its own colour.

The top and belly colours are important because the colour of the hair tip is obviously the most visible. The various top and belly colours are described in the colouring descriptions.

Dutch

Intermediate and base colour
After reading the above, it should be clear what is meant by intermediate and base colour. These colours can be seen by blowing into the coat. The hairs lay back, forming a kind of rosette that clearly shows the base, intermediate and topcoat colours.

Body condition and care
In this section the general impression that the rabbit makes will be judged. A dwarf rabbit should feel muscular and powerful. Sloppy, thin or fat animals will be judged poorly. Nails must be clipped, the coat clean and free of tangles. The eyes must be clean and bright. Sick or injured animals are marked down as extremely serious faults. Pregnant animals should not be shown.

Dwarf Lop

Netherland Dwarf with Himalayan pattern

It should be made clear that dwarf rabbits sold in pet shops are not always pure-bred rabbits. After all, they were bred as pets and not for showing. Often these are the most affectionate and good-natured animals.

Pet dwarf rabbits

Although most pet rabbits are not of a certain breed, we can still distinguish between a number of different types.

Most dwarf rabbits sold in pet shops are part or pure Lops. On a pure Lop, both ears droop. On a part-Lop one or one and a half ears will droop. Attention is needed here, as many different non-thoroughbred rabbits are crossed with one another to get rabbits with drooping ears.

Many a young dwarf rabbit has then grown to be a powerful giant with all the disappointment that involves.

The ears of a Dwarf Lop do not droop immediately at birth. During the first few weeks, they hang, stand or wave in the air or on the rabbit's back. On a real dwarf rabbit, the ears start to hang vertically beside the head over time. In the case of non-thoroughbred dwarf rabbits, there is always the question of how far the ears will actually droop. Sometimes one ear will droop, sometimes one and a half or half an ear. That (part of an) ear that does not droop then points right or left like some kind of traffic sign. This can look quite comical.

Breeds

Lion Head Rabbit

Lion Head Rabbit

These pet rabbits originally came from Germany, where they were called "Bearded Rabbit" or "Maned Rabbit". This is a more appropriate name. The Lion Head Rabbit, namely, has a crest of long hair around its head, something like a lion's mane. The tuft of hair between its ears is permanently raised. This long-eared variety is bred in all colours possible.

The mane on a Lion Head Rabbit is at its finest when it is young. Especially on fully grown males, the mane is less striking. That may be a good reason to get a female. In general, Lion Head Rabbits are soft-natured and quiet. Their character is indeed similar to that of the Dwarf Lop. Lion Head Rabbits are usually more expensive in pet shops than normal dwarf rabbits. Thoroughbred dwarf rabbits Apart from pet dwarf rabbits, there are the genuine thoroughbred dwarf rabbits. They come in three distinct and recognised breeds. In turn, these breeds have countless colourings and markings.

Dwarf Lop

The largest and most popular among the dwarf rabbits is the Dwarf Lop. It is a dwarf version of the French Lop and is present at all shows. Many different colours and patterns are bred.

The Dwarf Lop is friendly by nature and is striking for its typical form and ball-shaped head with drooping ears. It is presently recognised in most colours, including Agouti, Black, Blue, Seal Point, Sooty Fawn and White with red or blue eyes. The Broken Dwarf Lop is coloured with quite specific white marking. This breed is fairly fertile and generally has litters of four to five young.

The Polish

The Polish is a breed originating in England. It was originally only bred as an albino, which means white with red eyes. It is now bred in several colours and patterns, including Sable, Smoke, Otter, Fox and Blue Eyed White.

With a weight between eight hundred and a thousand grams, this is the smallest breed in the standard. The Polish we know today is quite different to the original Polish of the early years. Over the course of the years, it has become much more compact. Crosses between Polish rabbits with red and blue eyes produce variegated young similar to a heavy Dutch marking (a lot of black in the white). The Polish is known as being quite aggressive and is thus less suitable for children. This breed generally has no more than four young. Its ball-shaped head and extremely short ears makes the Polish an attractive animal.

Netherland Dwarf

The Netherland Dwarf's weight varies between eight hundred and one thousand grams. This breed is widely bred and is well represented at all shows. Although it is a popular breed, this is not thanks to its personality; the Netherland Dwarf is known as quite an awkward little character.

Netherland Dwarf rabbits are shown in quite a bewildering array of colours and patterns, including Agouti, Black, Blue, Smoke, Sable, and Otter. However, Red, Yellow and Chocolate are rare in the UK, as are Dutch-pattern and English-pattern Dwarfs.

Colourings

The list of colours has got you spinning and there were terms that, as a beginner, are totally unknown to you. Small animal breeders experiment a lot with different colours. It is often not easy to describe a colour exactly, because there are many nuances. This is why many colours are described precisely in the standard. Rabbits have to fulfil this standard to win prizes.

Agouti

This colour looks like that of the wild rabbit with black ticking. The colour should not be too dark. The belly is white with a blue base colour. The eyes are dark brown.

Cinnamon

This colour is almost identical to rabbit grey, but the ticking should be brown instead of black. The belly is white and the eyes are brown.

Opal

As rabbit grey, but with blue ticking. The belly is white with a blue under-colour and the eyes are blue-grey.

Black

The black has to be of a very intensive colour over the whole body. The belly may be a little lighter, and the eyes are dark brown.

Chocolate

In small animal breeding, chocolate is the colour of dark chocolate. The eyes are dark brown with a red glow, which can be difficult to see.

Blue

This colour is described as a shiny steel blue spread over the whole body. The eyes should be blue- grey.

Yellow

This is a warm yellow colour, without any black hair. The belly is white and the ears are pink.

Orange

This is a warm orange-red colour spread over the whole body. The colour is a little lighter on the belly. The eyes are dark brown.

Himalayan pattern

Tan markings

Polish albino

Chinchilla

This colour is named after the chinchilla, a South American rodent, related to the Guinea pig, with a superb coat. The mixed, black and light grey hair leads to an irregular ticking. This silver-grey colour covers almost the whole body. The eyes are blue.

Markings

Just as dwarf rabbits can have different colours, they can also have different markings.
A rabbit may have inherent markings and/or individual markings.

The standard distinguishes between the following markings:

Hotot

This is a white rabbit with black eye rings. The ring may be between three and five millimetres wide.

Harlequin

The Harlequin marking belongs to the breed of the same name. It is a mixed marking: one ear is dark or black, the other light. One side of the head is dark, the other light. The same applies to the paws.

Dutch marking

The back is striped red-black.

Dutch
This pattern, too, is named after a breed. A dwarf rabbit with this pattern has two identical patches over the head, each including the ear and the cheek. The ears are dark. The front of the body is white, the back darker. The front paws are white and the darker hind paws have a white ring.

Himalayan
The Himalayan pattern is also named after a breed. This white rabbit has dark points (tail, paws, ears and tip of nose). This pattern is also common on guinea pigs and fancy mice.

Silvering
For silvering, half of each hair is silver, which makes them appear to be jumping out. The silvering should be evenly spread. Besides the variable markings, there are also markings that are more strictly described. The following types are described in the standard:

Sooty Fawn
This consists of a yellow brown topcoat, with brown tips. This gives it a light red appearance which should not be too dark. The nose, breast, paws, ears and the lower part of the shoulders are dark. The basic colour of the belly is white to crème.

Hotot markings

Dutch pattern

Silver fox

The eyes and whiskers are dark brown.

Isabella
This pattern is lighter yellow in colour than the Madagascar. The hair tips are blue. The rest is the same as Sooty Fawn.

Silver fox
This pattern is named after the silver fox type of fur. A silver fox rabbit is dark with a white belly. The inside of the ears, an eye ring, a spot on the nose and a triangle in the neck are white. The so-called 'spots' are a speciality of the silver fox. These are bright white hairs on the animal's flanks, which become more dense the closer they are to the white belly. These spots give the animal its attractive appearance.

Tan
This is named after the breed with the same name, which was formerly known as 'black-and-tan'. A jet black rabbit with a fiery rust-red breast, belly and eye ring. The colour boundaries are clearly defined. Lighter coloured animals also have a lighter tan colour on the belly.

Coat structures
As we mentioned, besides the smooth-haired varieties, there are two other recognised coat structures.

Marten sable

Rex
This type of coat is named after a rabbit breed. The coat is very short and fine, just like a plush cuddly toy. It almost looks as if the rabbit has been sheared. This type of coat may be in any recognised colour.

Swiss Fox
A Swiss Fox rabbit has half-length white hair. The coat displays a lot of under-wool, whereby the hairs stand up. A boundary runs along the middle of the back. There the hairs fall somewhat to the sides, but they must not lay flat. The hairs must be three to five centimetres in length.

Black and tan

Whenever you keep a male and a female rabbit together, you are almost guaranteed offspring. You should think very carefully from the very beginning whether you really want to start breeding.

A litter of baby rabbits is very cute, but after the second and third time, it will be very difficult to find good homes for the babies. Therefore, be aware of all the aspects of reproduction when you buy your animals. If you have got a male and a female rabbit, but you do not want to breed, you must keep them in separate cages. It is also possible to have the male castrated.

Male or female
It is not easy to determine a (dwarf) rabbit's sex at a glance.

Experienced rabbit owners know a trick: They hold the rabbit upside down on their lap, and push the skin folds at the genital opening aside. A male rabbit will have a small penis. If you cannot tell the sex yourself, you can ask at a pet shop or vet's. It is quite common that a novice sales assistant makes a mistake in determining the sex, and the two 'females' all of a sudden have babies.

In-breeding
A responsible breeder will never mate just any male with any female, without first considering their ancestry, because of the risk of in-breeding. For example, if you've got a brother and sister from neighbours, it's best not to mate them. If these animals produce young, this is a

serious form of in-breeding and who can guarantee that the neighbour's litter wasn't also produced by a brother and a sister?

One occasion of in-breeding is certainly not a disaster, but several times in succession will quickly show the results. The young get smaller and weaker with each litter, fewer young are born and congenital abnormalities can also appear. However, in the right hands, careful in-breeding can be used to exaggerate and enhance certain characteristics. This is referred to as a 'strain'.

Mating

Spring is the best time to breed rabbits. A doe has to be in season before she can be covered. You can tell whether she is ready or not by her behaviour. She digs into the straw, builds nests and is generally very hectic. Do not let a strange buck into the doe's cage straight away. Put the cages next to each other for a few days, so that the animals can smell and see each other. Then put them together in a 'neutral' cage or (preferably) a room. The buck will try to win the doe over with lots of begging and macho-behaviour. The animals sniff each other intensively and the male licks the female.

He often runs around her grumbling, and lifting her tail. Finally, the female presses herself flat to the ground with her hindquarters raised. The actual mating process takes fifteen to twenty seconds. Try to plan for the birth, and therefore note the date when mating has taken place.

Pregnancy and birth

After successful mating, it takes approximately ten hours before the fertilised egg nestles into the uterus. The dwarf rabbit's pregnancy lasts approximately a month (between 28 and 32 days). The female will need plenty of rest in this period. She should no longer be picked up. She also needs extra feed and minerals. Give her a licking block, which contains salts and minerals. The mother-to-be knows instinctively what she needs to eat, and she will get the supplements she needs by licking the block. A few days before the birth, clean the cage thoroughly and offer plenty of nesting material. Once the doe has set up her nesting corner, this must naturally not be replaced.

The birth normally proceeds smoothly. The mother places the young in the nest, which she has prepared in advance by plucking her fur. Sometimes an inexperienced mother gives birth to her young in different parts of the cage, and leaves them to their fate.

In this case, place the young in the nest with the help of a cloth or a textile glove. Never touch the young with bare hands or leather gloves, as the mother may reject the young because of the scent.

After the birth, the mother will eat the afterbirth. This behaviour is instinctive and is a left-over from life in the wild. By eating the placenta, she takes in extra nutrients. It also prevents predators from smelling the afterbirth and attacking the young. Usually three to four young are born, but it can be up to eight. It is advisable to check for dead babies in the nest. Do this very carefully, as a threatened doe can be very aggressive towards humans and animals approaching her young.

Development

After the first check, you should leave the nest alone for a few days. Check again after four days. In most cases, the young will be lying in their nest with full bellies. Sometimes there's one animal left behind, which is obviously smaller and thinner. This animal will often survive, but will remain smaller and thinner. The first fur is visible after a few days. They open their eyes at around the tenth day. The young should grow quickly. Their weight will have doubled after a week, and after two weeks their weight is four times their birth-weight.

You can start to feed them after a month. Special food for young rabbits is available in pet shops.

Bottle-rearing
If the young remain thin and lean, the mother does not have enough milk. You can supplement it. If the mother dies after birth or rejects her young, you can try to rear them with a bottle yourself. This is only successful if they had their mother's milk after birth. You can buy small bottles designed for rearing kittens in the pet shop, which you can also use for rearing rabbits. Rabbits that have been raised with a bottle will be extremely affectionate, but the whole process is very time-consuming and laborious.

Depending on the mother's lactation, the babies have to be fed two to four times a day. After feeding, their bellies should be massaged with a damp Q-tip to encourage digestion. The mother does this by licking the bellies and genitals of her young.

There are a few general rules to follow whenever a dwarf rabbit is ill:
• If the animal lives together with other animals in the same cage, remove the sick animal as quickly as possible. It may be infectious and there is a risk to your other animals
• Place the sick animal in a quiet, darkened environment. Stress, crowding and noise are not good for recovery
• Do keep the animal warm, but make sure the surroundings are not too hot. The best temperature is 18 to 21° Celsius
• Don't wait too long before seeing a vet. Rabbits that are sick have little will to survive. Sometimes they die within a few days
• The patient must always have fresh water available. Remember that a sick animal might not be able to reach its water bottle
• Sick animals often eat little or nothing. Give it a small piece of apple or another (favourite) fruit.

Dwarf rabbits fortunately generally have few problems with their health. A healthy rabbit looks alert and is lively.

Its coat is smooth, soft and regular. The anal area is dry and clean. A sick dwarf rabbit always sits withdrawn. The coat is dull and stands up as if it were wet. The animal has a raised back, even when moving.

The old saying 'prevention is better than a cure' is especially true with small animals, such as rabbits. It is not always easy to treat a sick dwarf rabbit. Even a slight cold can be fatal for your dwarf rabbit. The biggest dangers are therefore draughts and damp.

On the page 48, you can see a few general rules you can follow if your dwarf rabbit is sick.

Colds and pneumonia

Draughts are among the most common cause of colds and pneumonia for dwarf rabbits, so choose the place for its home carefully. They can withstand low temperatures relatively well, but cold in combination with a draught almost inevitably leads to a cold. A rabbit starts sneezing and gets a wet nose. If its cold gets worse, the animal starts to breathe with a rattling sound and its nose will run even more, so it's now high time to visit the vet, who can prescribe antibiotics. A rabbit with a cold or pneumonia must be kept in a draught-free and warm room (18 to 21° C).

Health

Diarrhoea

Diarrhoea is another formidable threat to dwarf rabbits and often ends fatally. Unfortunately, diarrhoea is usually the result of incorrect feeding, sometimes in combination with draughts or damp. Some cases of diarrhoea are caused by giving the animal food with too high moisture content. Rotting food or dirty drinking water can also be a cause. You can do a lot yourself to prevent diarrhoea.

Should your rabbit become a victim then you must take any moist food out of the cage immediately. Feed your animal only dry bread, boiled rice or crispbread. Do not let the animal become dehydrated. Clean out its cage litter and nest material twice a day. As soon as the patient is completely recovered, you must disinfect its cage.
A cold or diarrhoea can be a pointer for one of the three dangerous rabbit diseases, coccidiosis, myxomatosis or snuffles. Because these diseases are extremely infectious and usually end in death, go to the vet immediately if you have any doubt.

Coccidiosis

This common intestinal disorder is a threat especially to young animals. They are very vulnerable at the age of six to eight weeks.

Coccidiosis is an illness which runs through several phases. It is caused by so-called 'oo-cysts' which are found in the mother's droppings. The young animal takes in these oo-cysts, which then change into coccidiosis in its intestines. This is made up of single-cell organisms that reproduce in the rabbit's intestines.

Bad hygiene, wrong ambient temperature and damp are major factors for the development of this illness. There are different types of coccidiosis. Symptoms include loss of weight and a bloated abdomen as a result of an intestinal infection. Early medical intervention can save the animal's life.

Myxomatosis victim

Broken back

Abscess of the jaw

Myxomatosis

Myxomatosis is one of the most common diseases amongst wild rabbits. It is spread via midges, fleas and ticks. At the beginning of an infection, the eyelids swell up. A gel-like fluid develops, which later turns into pus. The eyelids stick together very quickly and finally, the whole face swells up. An infected animal will die within ten days or so. This disease is basically not treatable. Preventive vaccination, however, is possible. If you keep your rabbits outdoors in an area where myxomatosis is prevalent, it is advisable to have them vaccinated.

Snuffles

Snuffles looks like a beginning cold, but can cause painful death within a few days. With this bacterial disease, bad hygiene and shelter (cold, draughty cages) play an important factor. Shortly after the first symptoms (sneezing and rattling), a watery excretion comes out of the nose. This excretion turns into pus, and the sneezing increases. At this point, a visit to the vet's is of utmost importance. If not treated, the rabbit will have trouble breathing and will die within a week. Snuffles develops very slowly, and affected animals lose a lot of weight. It is caused by a pastuerella infection and affected animals often sneeze at a very characteristic pitch.

Tumours

Dwarf rabbits are generally not particularly prone to tumours. If they do appear, it is usually at old age. Tumours are mostly found in families where a lot of in-breeding has occurred, in other words where members of the same family have been crossed with one another. The most common tumours affect the mammary glands of females. A tumour can also be the result of skin cancer. These forms can be removed surgically, but this might not be advisable because of the animal's advanced age.

Tumours can also be caused by an infection under the skin, which is called an abscess. A small wound may heal, but an infection can remain under the skin. This type of tumour can easily be treated by a vet who opens and cleans it. Should your rabbit show signs of a tumour, take It straight to the vet's. Delaying can only make things worse, both with skin cancer and abscesses.

Broken bones

Dwarf rabbits sometimes break bones because, being agile, they may jump off your hand or fall from a table. An animal with a broken paw will not put weight on it and will limp around the cage.

If it's a "straight" fracture (the paw is not deformed), this will heal within a few weeks. Take care that the rabbit can reach its food and drink without difficulty.

If a dwarf rabbit has broken its back, it's best to have it put to sleep. If in doubt about a possible fracture, always ask your vet.

Teeth malformations

Dwarf rabbits that are fed a diet with too few minerals run the risk of broken teeth. If you notice that your rabbit has a broken tooth, check that its diet is properly balanced. The vet can prescribe gistocal tablets to restore the calcium level. A broken front tooth will normally grow back, but you should check regularly that this is happening.

A rabbit's front teeth grow continuously and are ground down regularly by its gnawing. A genetic defect, a heavy blow or lack of gnawing opportunities can disrupt this process. Its teeth are ground irregularly and in the end don't fit together properly. In some cases the teeth continue to grow unchecked, even into the opposite jaw. When a rabbit's teeth are too long, it can no longer chew properly and the animal will lose weight and eventually starve to death.

Long teeth can easily be clipped back. A vet can show you how to do it.

Long teeth

Rabbit skull

Flea

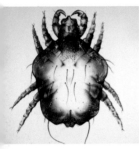

Mite

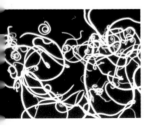

Worms

Parasites

Parasites are small creatures that live at the cost of their host. The best known are fleas on dogs and cats. Rabbits seldom have problems with parasites, and certainly not healthy animals. Weak, sick or poorly cared for animals, however, are far more likely to be affected. You mostly discover parasites only when an animal starts to scratch itself and gets bald patches. If you notice that your dwarf rabbit is itching and scratches itself frequently, then it's probably suffering from lice (tiny spiders that feed on blood). These lice are often spread by birds.

A pet shop or vet can advise you on dealing with parasites.

Fleas

There is a type of flea known as the rabbit flea, but the most common kind of flea found on rabbits are cat fleas. Rabbits are not especially vulnerable to them, because they don't particularly like a dense rabbit fur. If your other pets (especially cats and dogs) are free of fleas, then your rabbit will rarely have problems with them. But if your cat does suffer from fleas, then these will often make the jump to your rabbit. If you're treating a pet for fleas, then don't forget your rabbit(s). They are best treated with flea powder or spray. Make sure your rabbit cannot inhale it.

Skin mites or mange

The skin mite is a particularly harmful parasite. Fortunately they seldom occur, but if they do affect your dwarf rabbit, you've got work to do! The skin mite is a minute spider that creeps into its host's skin, making the mite itself almost never visible. It causes scabs and eczema, which can cover the whole skin within a month. Skin mites are infectious and can be passed on to other animals. Your vet or a good pet shop will have treatments for skin mites. Read the instructions on the packaging thoroughly. In most cases the infected animal must be bathed in the substance. Dry your dwarf rabbit off well to prevent it catching a cold and put it in a warm place (minimum 25° C).

Ear mites or mange

If your rabbit frequently shakes its head or holds it tilted, there's a good chance it's suffering from ear mites (or ear mange), which is also caused by tiny spiders. They feed on earwax and flakes of skin within the ear. The continuous irritation causes the ears to produce even more wax, causing the whole ear to fill with filth, which lead to serious itching. You can diagnose ear mites by simply looking into the ear. Your vet can prescribe an ear cleaner, which will take care of them immediately.

Worms

A dwarf rabbit can also suffer from a number of internal parasites. These are tiny organisms that live inside its body, such as worms and flukes. Worms and flukes are usually caught from dogs or wild rabbits, and are transferred by their droppings. If you pick grass for your rabbit in a place where dogs often run, or where wild rabbits live, this may hold this parasite's eggs. If your rabbit eats this grass, the eggs wind up in its stomach. Here they hatch and, slowly but surely, multiply. A rabbit with a worm infection may not directly become seriously ill, but will lose weight and be more vulnerable to other diseases, so be careful where you pick grass for your pet.

Fungal skin infections

Dwarf rabbits can sometimes suffer from fungal skin infections, which leave tiny flakes of skin in their ears and nose.
These infections are easily spread both to other animals and humans, but they are easy to treat. Don't let such infections go on too long, because they can lead to all kinds of other problems. Your vet has good treatments for fungal infections.

Old age

Obviously we hope that your pet will grow old without disease and pain. However, dwarf rabbits live nowhere near as long as humans and you must reckon with the fact that after just a few years you have an old rabbit to care for. Such an old rabbit will slowly become quieter and get grey hair in its coat, and now it needs a different kind of care. The time for wild games is over; it won't like them any more.
Leave your dwarf rabbit in peace. Dwarf rabbits, on average, live about five years. A seven-year old rabbit is very old. But, in exceptional cases they can reach the age of ten.

- Beware of contagious diseases.
- Never buy animals in badly run shops.
- Take a sample of its droppings when you go to the vet's.
- Take rotting food out of the cage. It can cause illness.
- Rabbits hate noise.
- Never let a rabbit nibble at house and garden plants.
- Offer your rabbit thistles and dandelion. It loves them!
- Never buy an animal that is too young.
- The importance of prevention not only applies to rabbits, but to all pets.
- Do not suddenly pull your hand back if your rabbit nibbles at it.
- Choose good bedding. Wood shavings often contain dust.
- Beware of insecticides. If in doubt, wash any fresh food.
- Draughts, damp, rotting or incorrect food, inadequate living space and overpopulation are factors which can affect your rabbit's health. Prevent them.
- Let your rabbit run free before feeding time. You can then lure it back with a treat.
- Isolate a patient suffering from a contagious disease.
- Never feed your rabbit with sweets, cake or salty foods. It can get ill.
- Check the droppings when buying a rabbit.
- Never buy a rabbit on the spur of the moment.
- Make sure that food and water bowls cannot tip over.
- A rabbit is not a rodent.
- Put a paving slab into your rabbit's cage. This will help to keep its nails short.
- Visit a small animal show.
- Check the ears before you buy a dwarf rabbit.
- Don't buy animals at a car-boot sale.

Dwarf Rabbit

A great deal of information can be found on the internet.

A selection of websites with interesting details and links to other sites and pages is listed here. Sometimes pages move to another site or address. You can find more sites by using the available search engine.

www.rabbitrehome.org.uk
At Rabbit Rehome UK rescue centres and individuals can enter details of rabbits in need of new homes and rabbit lovers can search for the rabbit that suits them best.

www.bunnymail.co.uk
Online-store. All you need for your rabbit on toys, grooming, accessories, foods and more.

www.homepage.mac.com/ mattocks/morfz/home.html
A website with lots of information on all topics related to rabbits. A great website.

www.carrotcafe.com
This website attempts to explain rabbit nutrition and feeding, not by telling you how to feed your bunny, but by telling you why you feed your bunny.

www.rabbitworld.com
Here you can find rabbit information on environment, diet, health and more.

www.tomatinstud.com
Another very informative website on rabbits, with lots of rabbit topics for breeders and fanciers.

Internet

British Small Animal Veterinary Association.
Woodrow House,
1 Telford Way, Waterwells Business Park, Quedgeley, Gloucester, GL2 2AB.
Telephone 01452 726700,
Administration e-mail:
adminoff@bsava.com
www.bsava.com

The Rabbit and Rodent Enthusiast Club
The R.R.E.C exists to promote kindness and understanding to rabbits and rodents, whilst at the same time, through their magazine, Nibbling News, educating their members on the care required by the animals that so enrich their lives.
The RREC, PO Box 741, Ampthill, MK45 1WZ

Rabbit Welfare Association
RWF, PO Box 603, Horsham, West Sussex RH13 5WL. National helpline - 01403 267658
www.houserabbit.co.uk

The British Rabbit Councel
This site has been designed for all members and anyone who is interested in exhibiting rabbits as a hobby or loves their pet rabbit.
info@thebrc.org
www.thebrc.org

The Rabbit Welfare Project website
Amongst other things, the Rabbit Welfare Project aims to improve rabbit welfare and knowledge, and to re-home unwanted rabbits.
www.welcome.to/rabbitproject

The House Rabbit Society
The House Rabbit Society is an all-volunteer, non-profit organisation situated in the USA that rescues abandoned rabbits and educates the public on rabbit care.
membership@rabbit.org
www.rabbit.org

Name:	Dwarf Rabbit
Latin name:	*Oryctolagus cuniculus*
Origin:	England
Body length:	25 - 35 cm
Tail length:	3 - 5 cm
Ear length:	5 cm (Polish/Netherland Dwarf) to max. 27 cm (Dwarf Lop)
Weight:	800 - 1650 grams (all breeds)
Body temperature:	37°C
Sexually mature:	7 months
Ready to breed:	7 months
Pregnancy:	28 - 31 days
Number of young:	3 - 4 (max. 8)
Birth weight:	45 - 70 grams
Eyes open:	after 10 days
Lactation period:	6 - 8 weeks
Life expectancy:	5 - 7 years

The Dwarf Rabbit